How to use this book

In this book, you will be able to practice and master your handwriting skills and develop your vocabulary over the two sections inside.

In the first section, you will work through the alphabet, practising your technique through repetition and ensuring you are up to speed with all of the letters in the English alphabet.

In the second section, you will practice your handwriting further by writing whole words that will refine your handwriting and introduce you to tricky words you may not have seen before (it's a great idea to put these in your BT Academy Vocab Journal!).

Whether you're using a pen or pencil, it's very important to spend some time finding the right pressure to use (which is how hard you push your writing tool into the paper whilst writing). Make sure you don't press too hard or too lightly whilst writing.

You'll usually be able to tell where this is when you can clearly make out each letter, but your pencil still feels as though it is gliding smoothly along the paper.

We recommend you really take your time at first and go slow. Focus on being smooth and consistent, meaning each letter of a type has a similar size and shape and fits in the provided guidelines. You should naturally speed up as you work through this book, so don't worry about being too slow!

Have fun!

Vocabulary Handwriting - Book 1

For specific queries or to report a printing error, please email:
contact@brilliant-tutors.co.uk

More from
Brilliant Tutors Academy

We have loads more to offer on our website:

www.brilliant-tutors.co.uk

Shop our 11+ courses taught by expert tutors, our ultra-realistic online and physical mock exams, and much more. We can't wait to see you there!

Vocabulary Handwriting - Book 1

For specific queries or to report a printing error, please email:
contact@brilliant-tutors.co.uk

More from
Brilliant Tutors Academy

We have loads more to offer on our website:

www.brilliant-tutors.co.uk

Shop our 11+ courses taught by expert tutors, our ultra-realistic online and physical mock exams, and much more. We can't wait to see you there!

HANDWRITING PRACTICE

HANDWRITING PRACTICE

a

a a a a a a a

a a a a a a

a a a a a a a a

a a a a a a a a

Write the letter in these empty boxes.

a a a a a a a

Trace the connecting letters and write them in the empty boxes.

a a a a a a a

HANDWRITING PRACTICE

b

Trace the letter on these dotted lines.

b b b b b b

b b b b b b

b

b b b b b b b b

b b b b b b b b

Write the letter in these empty boxes.

b b b b b b

b

Trace the connecting letters and write them in the empty boxes.

b b b b b b

b

HANDWRITING PRACTICE

C

c	c	c	c	c	c		C
c	c	c	c	c	c		
c	c	c	c	c	c	c	c
c	c	c	c	c	c	c	c

Write the letter in these empty boxes.

c	c	c	c	c	c		C

Trace the connecting letters and write them in the empty boxes.

c	c	c	c	c	c		C

HANDWRITING PRACTICE

d

d   d   d   d   d   d   d

d   d   d   d   d   d

d   d   d   d   d   d   d   d

d   d   d   d   d   d   d   d

Write the letter in these empty boxes.

d   d   d   d   d   d   d

Trace the connecting letters and write them in the empty boxes.

d   d   d   d   d   d   d

© BT ACADEMY

HANDWRITING PRACTICE

e

Trace the letter on these dotted lines.

e e e e e e e

e e e e e e

e e e e e e e e

e e e e e e e e

Write the letter in these empty boxes.

e e e e e e

e

Trace the connecting letters and write them in the empty boxes.

e e e e e e

e

HANDWRITING PRACTICE

f

Trace the letter on these dotted lines.

f   f   f   f   f   f   f

f   f   f   f   f   f

f   f   f   f   f   f   f   f

f   f   f   f   f   f   f   f

Write the letter in these empty boxes.

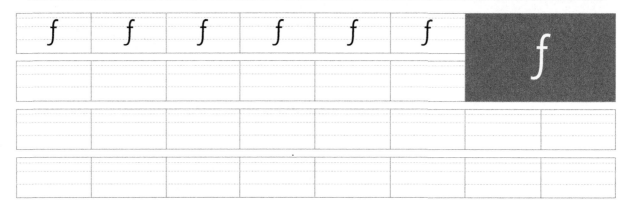

f   f   f   f   f   f   f

Trace the connecting letters and write them in the empty boxes.

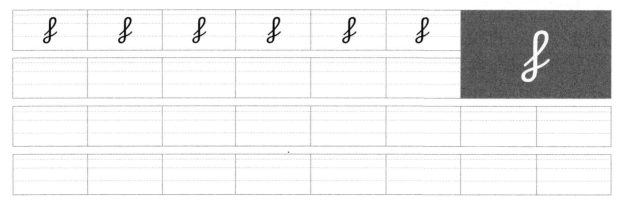

f   f   f   f   f   f   f

HANDWRITING PRACTICE

g

Trace the letter on these dotted lines.

g g g g g g

g

g g g g g g

g

g g g g g g g g

g g g g g g g g

Write the letter in these empty boxes.

g g g g g g

g

Trace the connecting letters and write them in the empty boxes.

g g g g g g

g

HANDWRITING PRACTICE

h

h   h   h   h   h   h   h

h   h   h   h   h   h

h   h   h   h   h   h   h   h

h   h   h   h   h   h   h   h

Write the letter in these empty boxes.

h   h   h   h   h   h   h

Trace the connecting letters and write them in the empty boxes.

h   h   h   h   h   h   h

HANDWRITING PRACTICE

i

i i i i i i
i
i i i i i i
i i i i i i i i
i i i i i i i i

Write the letter in these empty boxes.

i i i i i i
i

Trace the connecting letters and write them in the empty boxes.

i i i i i i
i

© BT ACADEMY

HANDWRITING PRACTICE

j

Trace the letter on these dotted lines.

j   j   j   j   j   j

j

j   j   j   j   j   j

j   j   j   j   j   j   j   j

j   j   j   j   j   j   j   j

Write the letter in these empty boxes.

j   j   j   j   j   j

j

Trace the connecting letters and write them in the empty boxes.

j   j   j   j   j   j

j

HANDWRITING PRACTICE

k

Trace the letter on these dotted lines.

k k k k k k

k

k k k k k k

k k k k k k k k

k k k k k k k k

Write the letter in these empty boxes.

k k k k k k

k

Trace the connecting letters and write them in the empty boxes.

k k k k k k

k

HANDWRITING PRACTICE

l

Trace the letter on these dotted lines.

Write the letter in these empty boxes.

Trace the connecting letters and write them in the empty boxes.

HANDWRITING PRACTICE

m

Trace the letter on these dotted lines.

m	m	m	m	m	m	m
m	m	m	m	m	m	
m	m	m	m	m	m	m	m
m	m	m	m	m	m	m	m

Write the letter in these empty boxes.

m	m	m	m	m	m	m

Trace the connecting letters and write them in the empty boxes.

m	m	m	m	m	m	m

HANDWRITING PRACTICE

n

n n n n n n
n
n n n n n n
n n n n n n n n
n n n n n n n n

Write the letter in these empty boxes.

n n n n n n
n

Trace the connecting letters and write them in the empty boxes.

n n n n n n
n

© BT ACADEMY

HANDWRITING PRACTICE

O

Trace the letter on these dotted lines.

O   O   O   O   O   O

O   O   O   O   O   O

O

O   O   O   O   O   O   O   O

O   O   O   O   O   O   O   O

Write the letter in these empty boxes.

O   O   O   O   O   O

O

Trace the connecting letters and write them in the empty boxes.

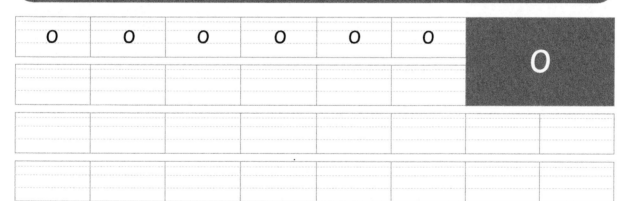

o   *o*   *o*   *o*   *o*   *o*

o

HANDWRITING PRACTICE

p

p   p   p   p   p   p   p

p   p   p   p   p   p   p

p   p   p   p   p   p   p   p

p   p   p   p   p   p   p   p

Write the letter in these empty boxes.

p   p   p   p   p   p   p

Trace the connecting letters and write them in the empty boxes.

p   p   p   p   p   p   p

© BT ACADEMY

HANDWRITING PRACTICE

q

Trace the letter on these dotted lines.

q q q q q q q

q q q q q q

q q q q q q q q

q q q q q q q q

Write the letter in these empty boxes.

q q q q q q

q

Trace the connecting letters and write them in the empty boxes.

q q q q q q

q

HANDWRITING PRACTICE

r

Trace the letter on these dotted lines.

r   r   r   r   r   r

r   r   r   r   r   r

r

r   r   r   r   r   r   r   r

r   r   r   r   r   r   r   r

Write the letter in these empty boxes.

r   r   r   r   r   r

r

Trace the connecting letters and write them in the empty boxes.

r   r   r   r   r   r

r

© BT ACADEMY

HANDWRITING PRACTICE

S

Trace the letter on these dotted lines.

S	S	S	S	S	S		
S	S	S	S	S	S	S
S	S	S	S	S	S	S	S
S	S	S	S	S	S	S	S

Write the letter in these empty boxes.

S	S	S	S	S	S		S

Trace the connecting letters and write them in the empty boxes.

S	S	S	S	S	S		S

HANDWRITING PRACTICE

t

Trace the letter on these dotted lines.

t	t	t	t	t	t	t
t	t	t	t	t	t	t
t	t	t	t	t	t	t	t
t	t	t	t	t	t	t	t

Write the letter in these empty boxes.

t	t	t	t	t	t	t

Trace the connecting letters and write them in the empty boxes.

t	t	t	t	t	t	t

HANDWRITING PRACTICE

u

u   u   u   u   u   u

u

u   u   u   u   u   u

u   u   u   u   u   u   u   u

u   u   u   u   u   u   u   u

Write the letter in these empty boxes.

u   u   u   u   u   u

u

Trace the connecting letters and write them in the empty boxes.

u   u   u   u   u   u

u

HANDWRITING PRACTICE

V

V	V	V	V	V	V	
V	V	V	V	V	V	V
V	V	V	V	V	V	V

V

Write the letter in these empty boxes.

V	V	V	V	V	V	

V

Trace the connecting letters and write them in the empty boxes.

N	N	N	N	N	N	

N

HANDWRITING PRACTICE

W

Trace the letter on these dotted lines.

W	W	W	W	W	W	W
W	W	W	W	W	W	
W	W	W	W	W	W	W
W	W	W	W	W	W	W

Write the letter in these empty boxes.

W	W	W	W	W	W	W

Trace the connecting letters and write them in the empty boxes.

W	W	W	W	W	W	W

HANDWRITING PRACTICE

X

X	X	X	X	X	X		X
X	X	X	X	X	X		
X	X	X	X	X	X	X	X
X	X	X	X	X	X	X	X

Write the letter in these empty boxes.

X	X	X	X	X	X		X

Trace the connecting letters and write them in the empty boxes.

X	X	X	X	X	X		X

HANDWRITING PRACTICE

y

Trace the letter on these dotted lines.

y y y y y y

y

y y y y y y

y y y y y y y y

y y y y y y y y

Write the letter in these empty boxes.

y y y y y y

y

Trace the connecting letters and write them in the empty boxes.

y y y y y y

y

HANDWRITING PRACTICE

Z

Trace the letter on these dotted lines.

Z Z Z Z Z Z

Z Z Z Z Z Z

Z Z Z Z Z Z Z Z

Z Z Z Z Z Z Z Z

Z

Write the letter in these empty boxes.

Z Z Z Z Z Z

Z

Trace the connecting letters and write them in the empty boxes.

Jz Jz Jz Jz Jz Jz

Jz

HANDWRITING PRACTICE
A

Trace the letter on these dotted lines.

A A A A A A
A

A A A A A A
A

A A A A A A A A

A A A A A A A A

Write the letter in these empty boxes.

A A A A A A
A

Trace the connecting letters and write them in the empty boxes.

Aa Aa Aa Aa Aa Aa
Aa

HANDWRITING PRACTICE

B

Trace the letter on these dotted lines.

B   B   B   B   B   B   B

B   B   B   B   B   B   B

B   B   B   B   B   B   B   B

B   B   B   B   B   B   B   B

Write the letter in these empty boxes.

B   B   B   B   B   B

B

Trace the connecting letters and write them in the empty boxes.

Bb   Bb   Bb   Bb   Bb   Bb

Bb

HANDWRITING PRACTICE

C

Trace the letter on these dotted lines.

C C C C C C | C

C C C C C C | C

C C C C C C C C

C C C C C C C C

Write the letter in these empty boxes.

C C C C C C | C

Trace the connecting letters and write them in the empty boxes.

Cc Cc Cc Cc Cc Cc | Cc

HANDWRITING PRACTICE

D

Trace the letter on these dotted lines.

D D D D D D

D D D D D D

D D D D D D D D

D D D D D D D D

D

Write the letter in these empty boxes.

D D D D D D

D

Trace the connecting letters and write them in the empty boxes.

Dd Dd Dd Dd Dd Dd

Dd

HANDWRITING PRACTICE E

Trace the letter on these dotted lines.

E E E E E E
E E E E E E
E E E E E E E E
E E E E E E E E

Write the letter in these empty boxes.

E E E E E E E

Trace the connecting letters and write them in the empty boxes.

Ee Ee Ee Ee Ee Ee Ed

HANDWRITING PRACTICE

Trace the letter on these dotted lines.

F	F	F	F	F	F	
F	F	F	F	F	F	**F**
F	F	F	F	F	F	F	F
F	F	F	F	F	F	F	F

Write the letter in these empty boxes.

F	F	F	F	F	F	
						F

Trace the connecting letters and write them in the empty boxes.

Fℓ	Fℓ	Fℓ	Fℓ	Fℓ	Fℓ	
						Fℓ

HANDWRITING PRACTICE

G

Trace the letter on these dotted lines.

G   G   G   G   G   G

G   G   G   G   G   G

G

G   G   G   G   G   G   G   G

G   G   G   G   G   G   G   G

Write the letter in these empty boxes.

G   G   G   G   G   G

G

Trace the connecting letters and write them in the empty boxes.

Gg   Gg   Gg   Gg   Gg   Gg

Gg

HANDWRITING PRACTICE

H

Trace the letter on these dotted lines.

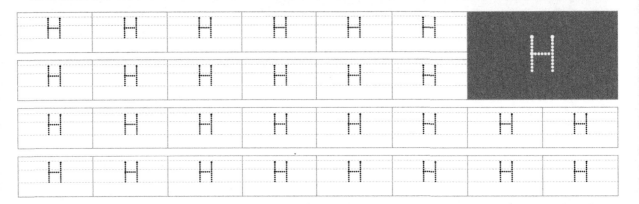

Write the letter in these empty boxes.

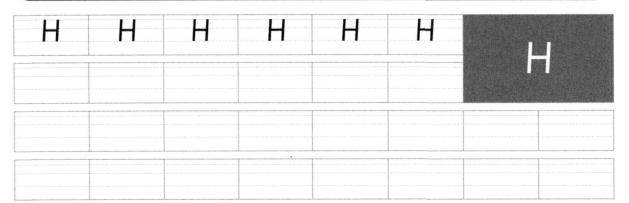

H

Trace the connecting letters and write them in the empty boxes.

Hh   Hh   Hh   Hh   Hh   Hh

Hh

HANDWRITING PRACTICE

I

Trace the letter on these dotted lines.

I I I I I I
I

I I I I I I

I I I I I I I I

I I I I I I I I

Write the letter in these empty boxes.

I I I I I I
I

Trace the connecting letters and write them in the empty boxes.

Ii Ii Ii Ii Ii Ii
Ii

HANDWRITING PRACTICE

Trace the letter on these dotted lines.

J   J   J   J   J   J   J

J   J   J   J   J   J

J   J   J   J   J   J   J   J

J   J   J   J   J   J   J   J

Write the letter in these empty boxes.

J   J   J   J   J   J   J

Trace the connecting letters and write them in the empty boxes.

Jj   Jj   Jj   Jj   Jj   Jj   Jj

© BT ACADEMY

HANDWRITING PRACTICE

Trace the letter on these dotted lines.

K	K	K	K	K	K	**K**
K	K	K	K	K	K	
K	K	K	K	K	K	K	K
K	K	K	K	K	K	K	K

Write the letter in these empty boxes.

| K | K | K | K | K | K | **K** |

Trace the connecting letters and write them in the empty boxes.

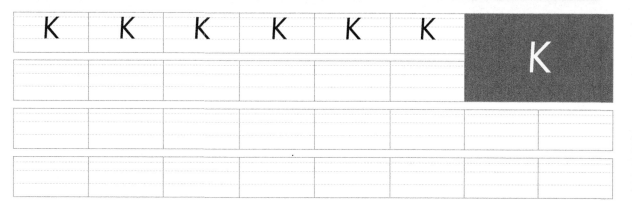

Kk   Kk   Kk   Kk   Kk   Kk   **Kk**

HANDWRITING PRACTICE

L

Trace the letter on these dotted lines.

L   L   L   L   L   L

L   L   L   L   L   L

L   L   L   L   L   L   L

L   L   L   L   L   L   L

Write the letter in these empty boxes.

L   L   L   L   L   L   L

Trace the connecting letters and write them in the empty boxes.

Ll   Ll   Ll   Ll   Ll   Ll   Ll

HANDWRITING PRACTICE

M

Trace the letter on these dotted lines.

M	M	M	M	M	M	
M	M	M	M	M	M	M

M

M	M	M	M	M	M	M	M
M	M	M	M	M	M	M	M

Write the letter in these empty boxes.

M	M	M	M	M	M	

M

Trace the connecting letters and write them in the empty boxes.

Mm	Mm	Mm	Mm	Mm	Mm	

Mm

HANDWRITING PRACTICE

N

Trace the letter on these dotted lines.

N N N N N N | N

N N N N N N

N N N N N N N N

N N N N N N N N

Write the letter in these empty boxes.

N N N N N N | N

Trace the connecting letters and write them in the empty boxes.

Nn Nn Nn Nn Nn Nn | Nn

HANDWRITING PRACTICE

O O O O O O O

O O O O O O O

O O O O O O O O

O O O O O O O O

O O O O O O O

Oσ Oσ Oσ Oσ Oσ Oσ Oσ

HANDWRITING PRACTICE

P

Trace the letter on these dotted lines.

P	P	P	P	P	P	
P	P	P	P	P	P	

P

P	P	P	P	P	P	P	P
P	P	P	P	P	P	P	P

Write the letter in these empty boxes.

P	P	P	P	P	P	

P

Trace the connecting letters and write them in the empty boxes.

Pp	Pp	Pp	Pp	Pp	Pp	

Pp

HANDWRITING PRACTICE

Q

Trace the letter on these dotted lines.

Q Q Q Q Q Q

Q Q Q Q Q Q

Q Q Q Q Q Q Q Q

Q Q Q Q Q Q Q Q

Q

Write the letter in these empty boxes.

Q Q Q Q Q Q

Q

Trace the connecting letters and write them in the empty boxes.

Qq Qq Qq Qq Qq Qq

Qq

HANDWRITING PRACTICE

R

Trace the letter on these dotted lines.

R R R R R R R

R R R R R R

R R R R R R R R

R R R R R R R R

Write the letter in these empty boxes.

R R R R R R

R

Trace the connecting letters and write them in the empty boxes.

Rr Rr Rr Rr Rr Rr

Rr

HANDWRITING PRACTICE

S

Trace the letter on these dotted lines.

S S S S S S S

S S S S S S S

S S S S S S S S

S S S S S S S S

Write the letter in these empty boxes.

S S S S S S S

Trace the connecting letters and write them in the empty boxes.

Ss Ss Ss Ss Ss Ss Ss

HANDWRITING PRACTICE

T

Trace the letter on these dotted lines.

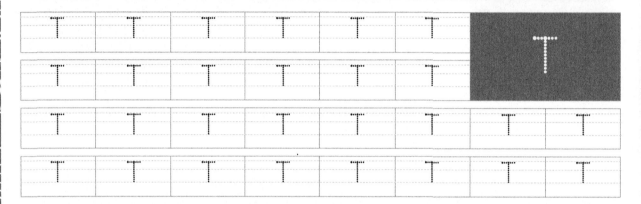

Write the letter in these empty boxes.

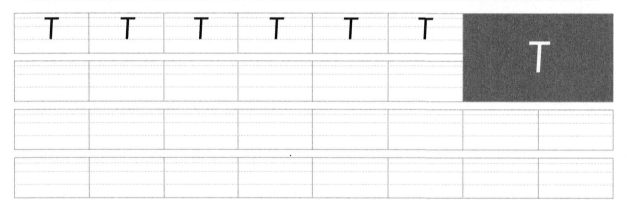

Trace the connecting letters and write them in the empty boxes.

Tt Tt Tt Tt Tt Tt

Tt

© BT ACADEMY

HANDWRITING PRACTICE

Trace the letter on these dotted lines.

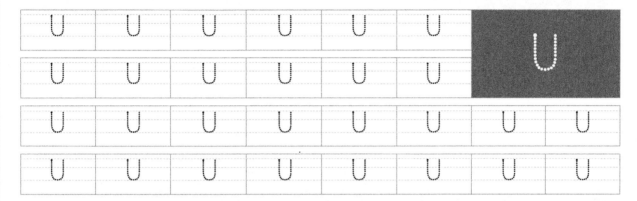

Write the letter in these empty boxes.

U U U U U U

U

Trace the connecting letters and write them in the empty boxes.

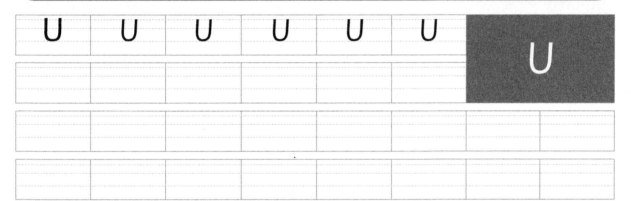

HANDWRITING PRACTICE   V

Trace the letter on these dotted lines.

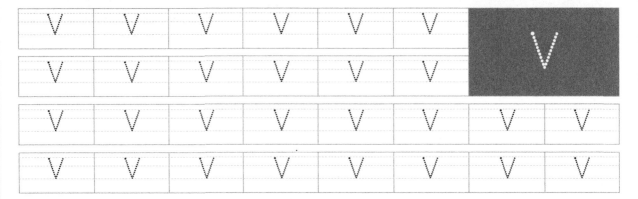

Write the letter in these empty boxes.

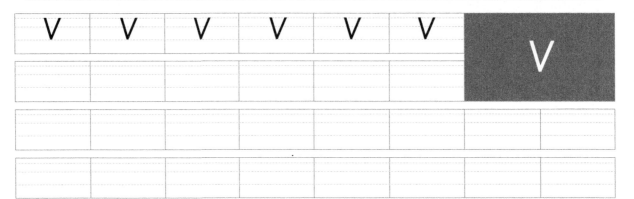

Trace the connecting letters and write them in the empty boxes.

© BT ACADEMY

HANDWRITING PRACTICE

W

Trace the letter on these dotted lines.

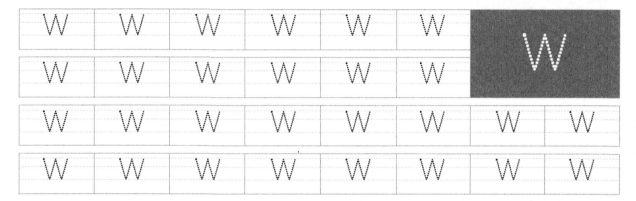

Write the letter in these empty boxes.

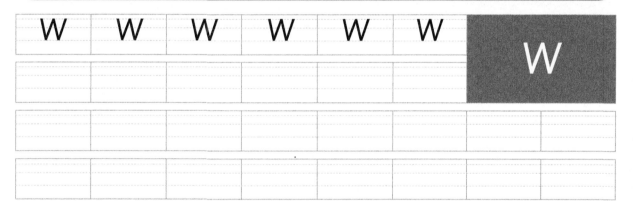

Trace the connecting letters and write them in the empty boxes.

© BT ACADEMY

HANDWRITING PRACTICE

Trace the letter on these dotted lines.

X X X X X X

X

X X X X X X

X X X X X X X X

X X X X X X X X

Write the letter in these empty boxes.

X X X X X X

X

Trace the connecting letters and write them in the empty boxes.

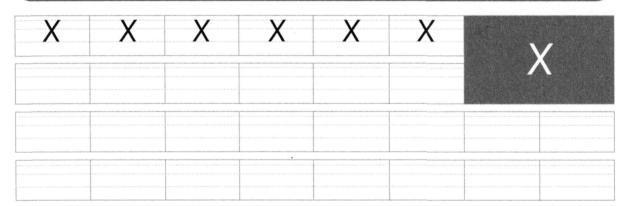

Xx Xx Xx Xx Xx Xx

Xx

HANDWRITING PRACTICE

Y

Trace the letter on these dotted lines.

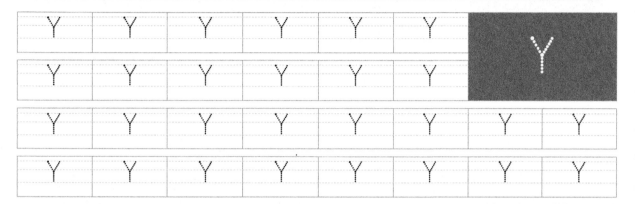

Write the letter in these empty boxes.

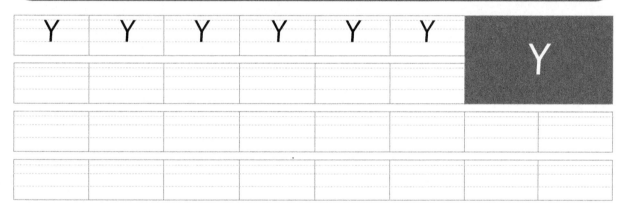

Trace the connecting letters and write them in the empty boxes.

Yy Yy Yy Yy Yy Yy   Yy

© BT ACADEMY

HANDWRITING PRACTICE

Z

Trace the letter on these dotted lines.

Z Z Z Z Z Z

Z Z Z Z Z Z

Z Z Z Z Z Z Z Z

Z Z Z Z Z Z Z Z

Z

Write the letter in these empty boxes.

Z Z Z Z Z Z

Z

Trace the connecting letters and write them in the empty boxes.

Zz Zz Zz Zz Zz Zz

Zz

VOCABULARY PRACTICE

Practise your weekly spelling words using continuous cursive handwriting

abandon abandon abandon

abase abase abase

abate abate abate

abbreviate abbreviate abbreviate

abdicate abdicate abdicate

aberrant aberrant aberrant

aberration aberration aberration

abet abet abet

abhor abhor abhor

abhorrent abhorrent abhorrent

abject abject abject

ablest ablest ablest

abode abode abode

abominable abominable abominable

abomination abomination abomination

Practise your weekly spelling words using continuous cursive handwriting

abrasive abrasive abrasive

abridge abridge abridge

abrupt abrupt abrupt

absence absence absence

absolute absolute absolute

absolution absolution absolution

absorb absorb absorb

absorbed absorbed absorbed

abstain abstain abstain

abstract abstract abstract

abstruse abstruse abstruse

absurd absurd absurd

abundance abundance abundance

abundant abundant abundant

abyss abyss abyss

Practise your weekly spelling words using continuous cursive handwriting

accelerate accelerate accelerate

accentuate accentuate accentuate

accessible accessible accessible

acclaim acclaim acclaim

accolade accolade accolade

accomplice accomplice accomplice

accusatory accusatory accusatory

accuse accuse accuse

accustom accustom accustom

acerbic acerbic acerbic

acquainted acquainted acquainted

acquiesce acquiesce acquiesce

acquiescence acquiescence acquiescence

acquire acquire acquire

acrimonious acrimonious acrimonious

Practise your weekly spelling words using continuous cursive handwriting

acrimony acrimony acrimony

acronym acronym acronym

across across across

acumen acumen acumen

acute acute acute

adamant adamant adamant

address address address

adept adept adept

adequately adequately adequately

adhere adhere adhere

adherent adherent adherent

adjacent adjacent adjacent

adjourn adjourn adjourn

adjudicate adjudicate adjudicate

admirable admirable admirable

Practise your weekly spelling words using continuous cursive handwriting

admission admission admission

adopt adopt adopt

adore adore adore

adorn adorn adorn

adulation adulation adulation

advance advance advance

advantageous advantageous advantageous

adversary adversary adversary

adverse adverse adverse

adversity adversity adversity

advocate advocate advocate

aesthetic aesthetic aesthetic

affable affable affable

affectionate affectionate affectionate

affinity affinity affinity

Practise your weekly spelling words using continuous cursive handwriting

affirmation affirmation affirmation

affliction affliction affliction

affluent affluent affluent

aggressor aggressor aggressor

aghast aghast aghast

agile agile agile

agitate agitate agitate

agnostic agnostic agnostic

agreeable agreeable agreeable

aid aid aid

alacrity alacrity alacrity

albeit albeit albeit

alert alert alert

alienate alienate alienate

allay allay allay

Practise your weekly spelling words using continuous cursive handwriting

allegation allegation allegation

alleviate alleviate alleviate

alluring alluring alluring

allusion allusion allusion

ally ally ally

aloof aloof aloof

altercation altercation altercation

altitude altitude altitude

altruistic altruistic altruistic

amalgamate amalgamate amalgamate

amateur amateur amateur

ambiguous ambiguous ambiguous

ambition ambition ambition

ambivalence ambivalence ambivalence

ambivalent ambivalent ambivalent

Practise your weekly spelling words using continuous cursive handwriting

ambles ambles ambles

ambling ambling ambling

amend amend amend

amiable amiable amiable

amorphous amorphous amorphous

amount amount amount

amphibian amphibian amphibian

ample ample ample

amplify amplify amplify

amply amply amply

amusing amusing amusing

anagram anagram anagram

analogous analogous analogous

analogy analogy analogy

anarchist anarchist anarchist

Practise your weekly spelling words using continuous cursive handwriting

androgynous androgynous androgynous

anecdote anecdote anecdote

angst angst angst

anguish anguish anguish

animosity animosity animosity

annihilated annihilated annihilated

anomaly anomaly anomaly

anonymous anonymous anonymous

antagonistic antagonistic antagonistic

antidote antidote antidote

antipathy antipathy antipathy

antiquated antiquated antiquated

antiquity antiquity antiquity

antithesis antithesis antithesis

antonym antonym antonym

Practise your weekly spelling words using continuous cursive handwriting

anxious anxious anxious

apathetic apathetic apathetic

apathy apathy apathy

aphorism aphorism aphorism

apoplectic apoplectic apoplectic

appalling appalling appalling

appeal appeal appeal

appearance appearance appearance

appease appease appease

apprehension apprehension apprehension

apprehensive apprehensive apprehensive

apprise apprise apprise

approve approve approve

aquainted aquainted aquainted

arable arable arable

arbitrary arbitrary arbitrary

arbitrate arbitrate arbitrate

archaic archaic archaic

ardour ardour ardour

arduous arduous arduous

argument argument argument

arid arid arid

arouse arouse arouse

arrears arrears arrears

arrogance arrogance arrogance

artful artful artful

article article article

articulate articulate articulate

artisan artisan artisan

ascendancy ascendancy ascendancy

Practise your weekly spelling words using continuous cursive handwriting

ascent ascent ascent

ascertain ascertain ascertain

ascetic ascetic ascetic

askance askance askance

aspiration aspiration aspiration

aspire aspire aspire

assail assail assail

assemble assemble assemble

assented assented assented

assertion assertion assertion

assessment assessment assessment

assiduous assiduous assiduous

assistance assistance assistance

assuage assuage assuage

assurance assurance assurance

Practise your weekly spelling words using continuous cursive handwriting

astounding astounding astounding

astute astute astute

asunder asunder asunder

asylum asylum asylum

atrocious atrocious atrocious

attached attached attached

attain attain attain

attempt attempt attempt

attentive attentive attentive

attribute attribute attribute

audacious audacious audacious

augment augment augment

augmenting augmenting augmenting

auspicious auspicious auspicious

austere austere austere

Practise your weekly spelling words using continuous cursive handwriting

austerity austerity austerity

authentic authentic authentic

authoritarian authoritarian authoritarian

autonomous autonomous autonomous

available available available

avarice avarice avarice

average average average

aversion aversion aversion

avoid avoid avoid

avowed avowed avowed

awe awe awe

awkward awkward awkward

awry awry awry

axiom axiom axiom

baleful baleful baleful

Practise your weekly spelling words using continuous cursive handwriting

balk balk balk

banal banal banal

bane bane bane

banish banish banish

barbarian barbarian barbarian

bargain bargain bargain

barren barren barren

beam beam beam

beautiful beautiful beautiful

because because because

becoming becoming becoming

bedraggle bedraggle bedraggle

belated belated belated

belies belies belies

believe believe believe

Practise your weekly spelling words using continuous cursive handwriting

belittle belittle belittle

bellicose bellicose bellicose

belligerent belligerent belligerent

bemoan bemoan bemoan

bemused bemused bemused

benefactor benefactor benefactor

beneficent beneficent beneficent

benefit benefit benefit

benevolent benevolent benevolent

benign benign benign

bequeath bequeath bequeath

berate berate berate

bereft bereft bereft

beseech beseech beseech

besieged besieged besieged

Practise your weekly spelling words using continuous cursive handwriting

betray betray betray

between between between

bewildered bewildered bewildered

biased biased biased

bickering bickering bickering

bicycle bicycle bicycle

bipartisan bipartisan bipartisan

bittersweet bittersweet bittersweet

bland bland bland

blasphemous blasphemous blasphemous

blasphemy blasphemy blasphemy

blatant blatant blatant

blaze blaze blaze

bleak bleak bleak

bleats bleats bleats

Practise your weekly spelling words using continuous cursive handwriting

blemish blemish blemish

blight blight blight

blissful blissful blissful

boast boast boast

boastful boastful boastful

boisterous boisterous boisterous

bolster bolster bolster

bombastic bombastic bombastic

boon boon boon

boundary boundary boundary

box box box

braggart braggart braggart

brandish brandish brandish

brawn brawn brawn

bray bray bray

Practise your weekly spelling words using continuous cursive handwriting

brazen brazen brazen

breach breach breach

breadth breadth breadth

brevity brevity brevity

brief brief brief

Britain Britain Britain

broach broach broach

broad broad broad

brooding brooding brooding

bruise bruise bruise

brusque brusque brusque

brutality brutality brutality

buffer buffer buffer

burden burden burden

burgeon burgeon burgeon

© BT ACADEMY

Practise your weekly spelling words using continuous cursive handwriting

burnish burnish burnish

business business business

busk busk busk

buttress buttress buttress

cache cache cache

cacophony cacophony cacophony

cajole cajole cajole

calamity calamity calamity

calculating calculating calculating

callous callous callous

callow callow callow

camaraderie camaraderie camaraderie

candid candid candid

candidate candidate candidate

candour candour candour

Practise your weekly spelling words using continuous cursive handwriting

cantankerous cantankerous cantankerous

capitulate capitulate capitulate

capricious capricious capricious

captivating captivating captivating

careering careering careering

caricature caricature caricature

carnivorous carnivorous carnivorous

cataclysmic cataclysmic cataclysmic

catalyst catalyst catalyst

catastrophic catastrophic catastrophic

category category category

cathartic cathartic cathartic

caulking caulking caulking

caustic caustic caustic

caution caution caution

Practise your weekly spelling words using continuous cursive handwriting

cavalier cavalier cavalier

cavorting cavorting cavorting

cease cease cease

celestial celestial celestial

cemetery cemetery cemetery

censure censure censure

centripetal centripetal centripetal

cerebral cerebral cerebral

certitude certitude certitude

cessation cessation cessation

challenge challenge challenge

challenging challenging challenging

chameleon chameleon chameleon

chaos chaos chaos

chapped chapped chapped

Practise your weekly spelling words using continuous cursive handwriting

charismatic charismatic charismatic

charlatan charlatan charlatan

charming charming charming

charred charred charred

chastised chastised chastised

chauvinist chauvinist chauvinist

cherish cherish cherish

cherished cherished cherished

chicanery chicanery chicanery

choreographer choreographer choreographer

chortle chortle chortle

chromosomes chromosomes chromosomes

chronicle chronicle chronicle

circumspect circumspect circumspect

circumvent circumvent circumvent

Practise your weekly spelling words using continuous cursive handwriting

civility civility civility

clamour clamour clamour

clamp clamp clamp

clarity clarity clarity

clemency clemency clemency

clement clement clement

cliche cliche cliche

clientele clientele clientele

coagulate coagulate coagulate

coarse coarse coarse

coax coax coax

coerce coerce coerce

coercion coercion coercion

cogent cogent cogent

coherent coherent coherent

Practise your weekly spelling words using continuous cursive handwriting

cohesion cohesion cohesion

collaborate collaborate collaborate

collaboration collaboration collaboration

college college college

colloquial colloquial colloquial

collusion collusion collusion

colossal colossal colossal

colour colour colour

combat combat combat

combative combative combative

combination combination combination

combustion combustion combustion

comforting comforting comforting

comical comical comical

commemorate commemorate commemorate

Practise your weekly spelling words using continuous cursive handwriting

commence commence commence

commentary commentary commentary

commit commit commit

committee committee committee

commotion commotion commotion

communicate communicate communicate

community community community

commute commute commute

companion companion companion

company company company

comparable comparable comparable

compassion compassion compassion

compel compel compel

compelling compelling compelling

compensate compensate compensate

© BT ACADEMY

Practise your weekly spelling words using continuous cursive handwriting

competition competition competition

compile compile compile

complacent complacent complacent

complaisant complaisant complaisant

completely completely completely

complex complex complex

compliance compliance compliance

compliant compliant compliant

complicity complicity complicity

composed composed composed

composition composition composition

composure composure composure

comprehend comprehend comprehend

compulsion compulsion compulsion

compute compute compute

Practise your weekly spelling words using continuous cursive handwriting

comrade comrade comrade

conceal conceal conceal

conceited conceited conceited

conceivable conceivable conceivable

concentrated concentrated concentrated

concerted concerted concerted

conciliatory conciliatory conciliatory

concise concise concise

conclude conclude conclude

conclusion conclusion conclusion

conclusive conclusive conclusive

concoct concoct concoct

concordant concordant concordant

concur concur concur

condemn condemn condemn

Practise your weekly spelling words using continuous cursive handwriting

condemnation condemnation condemnation

condense condense condense

condescending condescending condescending

condescension condescension condescension

condolence condolence condolence

condone condone condone

conducive conducive conducive

conferred conferred conferred

confine confine confine

confiscate confiscate confiscate

confiscated confiscated confiscated

confiscation confiscation confiscation

conflict conflict conflict

conformity conformity conformity

confound confound confound

Practise your weekly spelling words using continuous cursive handwriting

confrontational confrontational confrontational

congeal congeal congeal

congenial congenial congenial

conjure conjure conjure

connoisseur connoisseur connoisseur

conscience conscience conscience

conscientious conscientious conscientious

conscious conscious conscious

consensus consensus consensus

consent consent consent

consenting consenting consenting

conserve conserve conserve

consideration consideration consideration

consist consist consist

consistency consistency consistency

© BT ACADEMY

Practise your weekly spelling words using continuous cursive handwriting

consolation consolation consolation

conspicuous conspicuous conspicuous

conspire conspire conspire

constant constant constant

constellation constellation constellation

constituent constituent constituent

constraint constraint constraint

construe construe construe

consume consume consume

consumption consumption consumption

contagious contagious contagious

contaminate contaminate contaminate

contemplate contemplate contemplate

contemporary contemporary contemporary

contempt contempt contempt

© BT ACADEMY

Practise your weekly spelling words using continuous cursive handwriting

contemptible contemptible contemptible

contemptuous contemptuous contemptuous

contend contend contend

content content content

contented contented contented

contentious contentious contentious

contest contest contest

contract contract contract

contradiction contradiction contradiction

contrast contrast contrast

contribute contribute contribute

contrite contrite contrite

contrition contrition contrition

contrived contrived contrived

conventional conventional conventional

Practise your weekly spelling words using continuous cursive handwriting

convert convert convert

convey convey convey

convict convict convict

conviction conviction conviction

convince convince convince

convoluted convoluted convoluted

copious copious copious

cordial cordial cordial

corpulence corpulence corpulence

correct correct correct

corroborate corroborate corroborate

corrosive corrosive corrosive

countenance countenance countenance

counteract counteract counteract

courageous courageous courageous

Practise your weekly spelling words using continuous cursive handwriting

covert covert covert

covet covet covet

coy coy coy

crafty crafty crafty

crass crass crass

craving craving craving

credence credence credence

credibility credibility credibility

credit credit credit

credo credo credo

credulous credulous credulous

crescendo crescendo crescendo

crest-fallen crest-fallen crest-fallen

criterion criterion criterion

croak croak croak

Practise your weekly spelling words using continuous cursive handwriting

crucial crucial crucial

crude crude crude

cryptic cryptic cryptic

csermon csermon csermon

cue cue cue

cull cull cull

culpable culpable culpable

cultivate cultivate cultivate

cumulative cumulative cumulative

cunning cunning cunning

cupidity cupidity cupidity

curate curate curate

curator curator curator

curb curb curb

curious curious curious

Practise your weekly spelling words using continuous cursive handwriting

curriculum curriculum curriculum

cursory cursory cursory

curt curt curt

curtail curtail curtail

custom custom custom

customary customary customary

cylindrical cylindrical cylindrical

cynic cynic cynic

cynicism cynicism cynicism

dale dale dale

dangle dangle dangle

darn darn darn

dated dated dated

daunt daunt daunt

dawdle dawdle dawdle

Practise your weekly spelling words using continuous cursive handwriting

dazzling dazzling dazzling

dearth dearth dearth

debacle debacle debacle

debase debase debase

debate debate debate

debilitate debilitate debilitate

debrief debrief debrief

debriefing debriefing debriefing

debris debris debris

debtor debtor debtor

debunk debunk debunk

debutante debutante debutante

decadent decadent deculent

deceit deceit deceit

deceive deceive deceive

Practise your weekly spelling words using continuous cursive handwriting

deciduous deciduous deciduous

decisive decisive decisive

declaim declaim declaim

declare declare declare

decline decline decline

declivity declivity declivity

decorous decorous decorous

decorum decorum decorum

decree decree decree

decry decry decry

deduction deduction deduction

deface deface deface

defamatory defamatory defamatory

defame defame defame

defective defective defective

deference deference deference

deferential deferential deferential

deferment deferment deferment

defiance defiance defiance

defiant defiant defiant

deficit deficit deficit

definite definite definite

deft deft deft

defy defy defy

degenerate degenerate degenerate

degradation degradation degradation

degrade degrade degrade

deject deject deject

delectable delectable delectable

delegate delegate delegate

Practise your weekly spelling words using continuous cursive handwriting

deleterious deleterious deleterious

deliberate deliberate deliberate

deliberation deliberation deliberation

delightful delightful delightful

delineate delineate delineate

delirious delirious delirious

delude delude delude

deluded deluded deluded

deluge deluge deluge

demagogue demagogue demagogue

demeanour demeanour demeanour

demolish demolish demolish

demolished demolished demolished

demolition demolition demolition

demonize demonize demonize

Practise your weekly spelling words using continuous cursive handwriting

demote demote demote

demotion demotion demotion

demur demur demur

demure demure demure

denigrate denigrate denigrate

denizen denizen denizen

denounce denounce denounce

deny deny deny

depict depict depict

deplore deplore deplore

deploy deploy deploy

depose depose depose

deposit deposit deposit

depot depot depot

depraved depraved depraved

depravity depravity depravity

deprecate deprecate deprecate

depressing depressing depressing

derail derail derail

deranged deranged deranged

derelict derelict derelict

deride deride deride

derision derision derision

derisive derisive derisive

derivative derivative derivative

derogate derogate derogate

description description description

desecrate desecrate desecrate

desecration desecration desecration

desiccate desiccate desiccate

Practise your weekly spelling words using continuous cursive handwriting

desire desire desire

desist desist desist

desolate desolate desolate

despair despair despair

desperately desperately desperately

despicable despicable despicable

despise despise despise

despised despised despised

despondent despondent despondent

despot despot despot

destitute destitute destitute

destitution destitution destitution

desultory desultory desultory

detached detached detached

detain detain detain

Practise your weekly spelling words using continuous cursive handwriting

determine determine determine

deterrent deterrent deterrent

detractor detractor detractor

detractors detractors detractors

detrimental detrimental detrimental

develop develop develop

device device device

devious devious devious

devise devise devise

devote devote devote

devour devour devour

dexterous dexterous dexterous

diabolical diabolical diabolical

diameter diameter diameter

diaphanous diaphanous diaphanous

Practise your weekly spelling words using continuous cursive handwriting

diatribe diatribe diatribe

dichotomy dichotomy dichotomy

diction diction diction

dictionary dictionary dictionary

diffident diffident diffident

diffuse diffuse diffuse

digest digest digest

dignity dignity dignity

digress digress digress

digression digression digression

dilapidated dilapidated dilapidated

dilate dilate dilate

diligence diligence diligence

diligent diligent diligent

diluted diluted diluted

Practise your weekly spelling words using continuous cursive handwriting

dim dim dim

diminish diminish diminish

diminution diminution diminution

din din din

dingy dingy dingy

diplomatic diplomatic diplomatic

disabuse disabuse disabuse

disappear disappear disappear

disappointed disappointed disappointed

disarray disarray disarray

disaster disaster disaster

disastrous disastrous disastrous

disavow disavow disavow

disband disband disband

discern discern discern

Practise your weekly spelling words using continuous cursive handwriting

discerning discerning discerning

disclose disclose disclose

discombobulated discombobulated discombobulated

discomfit discomfit discomfit

disconcert disconcert disconcert

discontent discontent discontent

discord discord discord

discordant discordant discordant

discordant discordant discordant

discourse discourse discourse

discourteous discourteous discourteous

discredit discredit discredit

discrepancy discrepancy discrepancy

discrete discrete discrete

discretion discretion discretion

© BT ACADEMY

Practise your weekly spelling words using continuous cursive handwriting

discretionary discretionary discretionary

discretionary discretionary discretionary

discriminating discriminating discriminating

discursive discursive discursive

disdain disdain disdain

dishevelled dishevelled dishevelled

disinclination disinclination disinclination

disingenuous disingenuous disingenuous

disintegrate disintegrate disintegrate

disinterested disinterested disinterested

dismal dismal dismal

dismantle dismantle dismantle

dismay dismay dismay

dismissal dismissal dismissal

disparage disparage disparage

Practise your weekly spelling words using continuous cursive handwriting

disparaging disparaging disparaging

disparate disparate disparate

disparity disparity disparity

dispassionate dispassionate dispassionate

dispel dispel dispel

disperse disperse disperse

display display display

disputatious disputatious disputatious

dispute dispute dispute

disregard disregard disregard

dissemble dissemble dissemble

disseminate disseminate disseminate

dissension dissension dissension

dissent dissent dissent

dissident dissident dissident

Practise your weekly spelling words using continuous cursive handwriting

dissipate dissipate dissipate

dissonance dissonance dissonance

dissuade dissuade dissuade

distant distant distant

distasteful distasteful distasteful

distend distend distend

distinct distinct distinct

distinctive distinctive distinctive

distinguished distinguished distinguished

distortion distortion distortion

distract distract distract

distress distress distress

distressing distressing distressing

disturbing disturbing disturbing

dither dither dither

Practise your weekly spelling words using continuous cursive handwriting

divergent divergent divergent

diverse diverse diverse

divert divert divert

divination divination divination

divine divine divine

divinity divinity divinity

divisive divisive divisive

divulge divulge divulge

docile docile docile

doctrine doctrine doctrine

dogma dogma dogma

dogmatic dogmatic dogmatic

dogmatic dogmatic dogmatic

domestic domestic domestic

dominant dominant dominant

Practise your weekly spelling words using continuous cursive handwriting

dormant dormant dormant

dose dose dose

double double double

doubtful doubtful doubtful

dour dour dour

doyen doyen doyen

drab drab drab

drawback drawback drawback

droll droll droll

drone drone drone

drought drought drought

drub drub drub

dual dual dual

dubious dubious dubious

dulcet dulcet dulcet

Practise your weekly spelling words using continuous cursive handwriting

dull dull dull

dumb dumb dumb

dupe dupe dupe

duplicate duplicate duplicate

duplicity duplicity duplicity

duration duration duration

duress duress duress

dutiful dutiful dutiful

dwelling dwelling dwelling

earnest earnest earnest

ebb ebb ebb

ebullient ebullient ebullient

eccentric eccentric eccentric

eclectic eclectic eclectic

eclipse eclipse eclipse

Practise your weekly spelling words using continuous cursive handwriting

economical economical economical

ecstasy ecstasy ecstasy

ecstatic ecstatic ecstatic

edible edible edible

edict edict edict

edify edify edify

efface efface efface

effervescent effervescent effervescent

efficacious efficacious efficacious

efficient efficient efficient

effigy effigy effigy

effusion effusion effusion

effusive effusive effusive

egotist egotist egotist

egotistical egotistical egotistical

egregious egregious egregious

egress egress egress

elate elate elate

elated elated elated

elect elect elect

elegy elegy elegy

elevated elevated elevated

eliminate eliminate eliminate

elocution elocution elocution

eloquence eloquence eloquence

eloquent eloquent eloquent

elucidate elucidate elucidate

elude elude elude

elusive elusive elusive

emanate emanate emanate

Practise your weekly spelling words using continuous cursive handwriting

embarrass embarrass embarrass

embellish embellish embellish

embezzle embezzle embezzle

embittered embittered embittered

embrace embrace embrace

embroiled embroiled embroiled

emerge emerge emerge

emigrate emigrate emigrate

eminent eminent eminent

emissary emissary emissary

emollient emollient emollient

empathy empathy empathy

emphasis emphasis emphasis

emphatic emphatic emphatic

empire empire empire

employ employ employ

emulate emulate emulate

enchant enchant enchant

enchanting enchanting enchanting

encompass encompass encompass

encroach encroach encroach

encumber encumber encumber

endeavour endeavour endeavour

endemic endemic endemic

endorse endorse endorse

endurance endurance endurance

endure endure endure

enduring enduring enduring

enervate enervate enervate

enforce enforce enforce

Practise your weekly spelling words using continuous cursive handwriting

enfranchise enfranchise enfranchise

engender engender engender

engrossed engrossed engrossed

enhance enhance enhance

enigma enigma enigma

enigmatic enigmatic enigmatic

enigmatic enigmatic enigmatic

enmity enmity enmity

ennui ennui ennui

enormity enormity enormity

enormousness enormousness enormousness

enrage enrage enrage

ensconce ensconce ensconce

entangle entangle entangle

entendre entendre entendre

Practise your weekly spelling words using continuous cursive handwriting

enterprise enterprise enterprise

enthralling enthralling enthralling

enthusiasm enthusiasm enthusiasm

entire entire entire

entirely entirely entirely

entreat entreat entreat

enumerate enumerate enumerate

environment environment environment

ephemeral ephemeral ephemeral

epic epic epic

epicure epicure epicure

epigram epigram epigram

epilogue epilogue epilogue

epiphany epiphany epiphany

episodic episodic episodic

© BT ACADEMY

Practise your weekly spelling words using continuous cursive handwriting

epitaph epitaph epitaph

epoch epoch epoch

eponym eponym eponym

eponymous eponymous eponymous

equanimity equanimity equanimity

equip equip equip

equipment equipment equipment

equipped equipped equipped

equitable equitable equitable

equivocal equivocal equivocal

equivocate equivocate equivocate

era era era

eradicate eradicate eradicate

erasable erasable erasable

erect erect erect

© BT ACADEMY

Practise your weekly spelling words using continuous cursive handwriting

erosion erosion erosion

errand errand errand

erratic erratic erratic

erroneous erroneous erroneous

erudite erudite erudite

eschew eschew eschew

esoteric esoteric esoteric

especially especially especially

espouse espouse espouse

essential essential essential

esteem esteem esteem

estimable estimable estimable

estimate estimate estimate

ethereal ethereal ethereal

ethical ethical ethical

Practise your weekly spelling words using continuous cursive handwriting

eulogy eulogy eulogy

euphemism euphemism euphemism

euphonious euphonious euphonious

euphoria euphoria euphoria

evade evade evade

evaluate evaluate evaluate

evaluation evaluation evaluation

evanescent evanescent evanescent

evaporate evaporate evaporate

evident evident evident

evince evince evince

exacerbate exacerbate exacerbate

exacting exacting exacting

exaggerate exaggerate exaggerate

exalt exalt exalt

Practise your weekly spelling words using continuous cursive handwriting

exasperate exasperate exasperate

excellent excellent excellent

exception exception exception

excitement excitement excitement

exciting exciting exciting

exclaim exclaim exclaim

exclude exclude exclude

excoriate excoriate excoriate

exculpate exculpate exculpate

excursion excursion excursion

exemplary exemplary exemplary

exemplify exemplify exemplify

exhaustive exhaustive exhaustive

exhilarating exhilarating exhilarating

exhort exhort exhort

Practise your weekly spelling words using continuous cursive handwriting

exhume exhume exhume

exigent exigent exigent

existence existence existence

exonerate exonerate exonerate

exorbitant exorbitant exorbitant

expedient expedient expedient

expedite expedite expedite

expel expel expel

expense expense expense

expertise expertise expertise

expiate expiate expiate

explanation explanation explanation

explicit explicit explicit

exploit exploit exploit

exponent exponent exponent

Practise your weekly spelling words using continuous cursive handwriting

expository expository expository

expound expound expound

expropriate expropriate expropriate

expunge expunge expunge

expurgate expurgate expurgate

exquisite exquisite exquisite

extemporaneous extemporaneous extemporaneous

extended extended extended

extensive extensive extensive

extenuating extenuating extenuating

exterior exterior exterior

exterminate exterminate exterminate

extinction extinction extinction

extol extol extol

extract extract extract

Practise your weekly spelling words using continuous cursive handwriting

extraneous extraneous extraneous

extraordinary extraordinary extraordinary

extrapolation extrapolation extrapolation

extravagant extravagant extravagant

extreme extreme extreme

extremely extremely extremely

extricate extricate extricate

extrinsic extrinsic extrinsic

extrovert extrovert extrovert

extroverted extroverted extroverted

extrude extrude extrude

exuberance exuberance exuberance

exultant exultant exultant

fabricated fabricated fabricated

facade facade facade

Practise your weekly spelling words using continuous cursive handwriting

facetious facetious facetious

facile facile facile

facilitate facilitate facilitate

fact fact fact

factual factual factual

fallacious fallacious fallacious

fallow fallow fallow

falsify falsify falsify

famine famine famine

fanatic fanatic fanatic

fanatical fanatical fanatical

fanaticism fanaticism fanaticism

fanfare fanfare fanfare

farcical farcical farcical

fastidious fastidious fastidious

Practise your weekly spelling words using continuous cursive handwriting

fatal fatal fatal

fateful fateful fateful

fathom fathom fathom

fatigue fatigue fatigue

fatuous fatuous fatuous

faux faux faux

favourite favourite favourite

favouritism favouritism favouritism

fawn fawn fawn

feasible feasible feasible

febrile febrile febrile

february february february

feckless feckless feckless

fecund fecund fecund

feeble feeble feeble

Practise your weekly spelling words using continuous cursive handwriting

feign feign feign

felicitous felicitous felicitous

femininity femininity femininity

feral feral feral

ferocity ferocity ferocity

fertile fertile fertile

fervid fervid fervid

fervour fervour fervour

fetid fetid fetid

fetter fetter fetter

fiasco fiasco fiasco

fickle fickle fickle

fidelity fidelity fidelity

figurative figurative figurative

filibuster filibuster filibuster

Practise your weekly spelling words using continuous cursive handwriting

filly filly filly

finesse finesse finesse

finite finite finite

firebrand firebrand firebrand

fission fission fission

flabbergast flabbergast flabbergast

flaccid flaccid flaccid

flag flag flag

flagrant flagrant flagrant

flagrant flagrant flagrant

flamboyant flamboyant flamboyant

flank flank flank

flattering flattering flattering

flatulence flatulence flatulence

flaunt flaunt flaunt

© BT ACADEMY

Practise your weekly spelling words using continuous cursive handwriting

flaw flaw flaw

flawed flawed flawed

flawless flawless flawless

flee flee flee

fleet fleet fleet

fleet fleet fleet

flimsy flimsy flimsy

flippancy flippancy flippancy

flippant flippant flippant

flora flora flora

florid florid florid

flourish flourish flourish

flout flout flout

fluctuate fluctuate fluctuate

foal foal foal

Practise your weekly spelling words using continuous cursive handwriting

fodder fodder fodder

foe foe foe

foible foible foible

foil foil foil

foment foment foment

foolhardy foolhardy foolhardy

forbearance forbearance forbearance

forbid forbid forbid

force force force

ford ford ford

forego forego forego

foremost foremost foremost

foreshadow foreshadow foreshadow

foresight foresight foresight

forestall forestall forestall

Practise your weekly spelling words using continuous cursive handwriting

forge forge forge

forgery forgery forgery

forlorn forlorn forlorn

formidable formidable formidable

forsake forsake forsake

forswear forswear forswear

forte forte forte

forthright forthright forthright

fortitude fortitude fortitude

fortuitous fortuitous fortuitous

forum forum forum

foster foster foster

foundation foundation foundation

fracas fracas fracas

fractious fractious fractious

Practise your weekly spelling words using continuous cursive handwriting

fragment fragment fragment

fragrant fragrant fragrant

frail frail frail

frantic frantic frantic

fraud fraud fraud

fraudulent fraudulent fraudulent

frenzy frenzy frenzy

frequency frequency frequency

frequent frequent frequent

friend friend friend

frightful frightful frightful

frivolous frivolous frivolous

frolicsome frolicsome frolicsome

front front front

frugal frugal frugal

Practise your weekly spelling words using continuous cursive handwriting

frugality frugality frugality

frugality frugality frugality

fugitive fugitive fugitive

fulfilled fulfilled fulfilled

fulsome fulsome fulsome

fund fund fund

furtive furtive furtive

furtively furtively furtively

futile futile futile

gallant gallant gallant

galvanise galvanise galvanise

galvanize galvanize galvanize

gambol gambol gambol

gamely gamely gamely

garbled garbled garbled

Practise your weekly spelling words using continuous cursive handwriting

gargantuan gargantuan gargantuan

garish garish garish

garment garment garment

garner garner garner

garrulous garrulous garrulous

gasket gasket gasket

gauche gauche gauche

gauge gauge gauge

genealogy genealogy genealogy

generalize generalize generalize

genial genial genial

genre genre genre

gentility gentility gentility

gestation gestation gestation

gibber gibber gibber

Practise your weekly spelling words using continuous cursive handwriting

gibe gibe gibe

glacier glacier glacier

glib glib glib

gloomy gloomy gloomy

glossy glossy glossy

glower glower glower

glutton glutton glutton

goad goad goad

goaded goaded goaded

gorge gorge gorge

government government government

gracious gracious gracious

gradation gradation gradation

grandeur grandeur grandeur

grandiose grandiose grandiose

© BT ACADEMY

Practise your weekly spelling words using continuous cursive handwriting

granular granular granular

grata grata grata

grate grate grate

gratifying gratifying gratifying

gratis gratis gratis

gratitude gratitude gratitude

gratuitous gratuitous gratuitous

gratuity gratuity gratuity

grave grave grave

gravel gravel gravel

gravity gravity gravity

gregarious gregarious gregarious

grievance grievance grievance

grieve grieve grieve

grievous grievous grievous

Practise your weekly spelling words using continuous cursive handwriting

gripe gripe gripe

grotesque grotesque grotesque

grotto grotto grotto

grudging grudging grudging

grudgingly grudgingly grudgingly

gruff gruff gruff

guarantee guarantee guarantee

guard guard guard

guile guile guile

gullible gullible gullible

gung-ho gung-ho gung-ho

guttural guttural guttural

habitable habitable habitable

habitat habitat habitat

hackneyed hackneyed hackneyed

© BT ACADEMY

Practise your weekly spelling words using continuous cursive handwriting

hallmark hallmark hallmark

hallowed hallowed hallowed

halt halt halt

hamper hamper hamper

handkerchief handkerchief handkerchief

handsome handsome handsome

hapless hapless hapless

harangue harangue harangue

harass harass harass

harbinger harbinger harbinger

harbour harbour harbour

hardy hardy hardy

harmonious harmonious harmonious

harrowing harrowing harrowing

haste haste haste

Practise your weekly spelling words using continuous cursive handwriting

hasty hasty hasty

haughtiness haughtiness haughtiness

haughty haughty haughty

hazardous hazardous hazardous

hearth hearth hearth

heartless heartless heartless

heckler heckler heckler

hedonist hedonist hedonist

heed heed heed

heeding heeding heeding

heedless heedless heedless

heinous heinous heinous

helix helix helix

heresy heresy heresy

heretical heretical heretical

© BT ACADEMY

Practise your weekly spelling words using continuous cursive handwriting

heroic heroic heroic

hesitant hesitant hesitant

heterogeneous heterogeneous heterogeneous

hiatus hiatus hiatus

hierarchical hierarchical hierarchical

hierarchy hierarchy hierarchy

hilarious hilarious hilarious

hinder hinder hinder

hindrance hindrance hindrance

hindsight hindsight hindsight

hinge hinge hinge

hinterland hinterland hinterland

histrionic histrionic histrionic

hoard hoard hoard

hoax hoax hoax

Practise your weekly spelling words using continuous cursive handwriting

hodgepodge hodgepodge hodgepodge

hoes hoes hoes

hoist hoist hoist

holiday holiday holiday

hollow hollow hollow

homogeneous homogeneous homogeneous

homograph homograph homograph

homonym homonym homonym

homophone homophone homophone

hone hone hone

hoof hoof hoof

horrendous horrendous horrendous

hospitable hospitable hospitable

hostile hostile hostile

hostility hostility hostility

© BT ACADEMY

Practise your weekly spelling words using continuous cursive handwriting

hubris hubris hubris

humane humane humane

humble humble humble

humorous humorous humorous

hybrid hybrid hybrid

hygienic hygienic hygienic

hyperbole hyperbole hyperbole

hypocrisy hypocrisy hypocrisy

hypocritical hypocritical hypocritical

hypothesis hypothesis hypothesis

hypothetical hypothetical hypothetical

idealist idealist idealist

idiom idiom idiom

idiosyncrasy idiosyncrasy idiosyncrasy

idle idle idle

© BT ACADEMY

idol idol idol

idyllic idyllic idyllic

ignominy ignominy ignominy

ignorant ignorant ignorant

illegible illegible illegible

illicit illicit illicit

illuminate illuminate illuminate

illusory illusory illusory

illustrate illustrate illustrate

imbalance imbalance imbalance

imbibe imbibe imbibe

imitate imitate imitate

immaculate immaculate immaculate

immediate immediate immediate

immediately immediately immediately

Practise your weekly spelling words using continuous cursive handwriting

immerse immerse immerse

imminent imminent imminent

immoderate immoderate immoderate

immoral immoral immoral

immunity immunity immunity

immutable immutable immutable

impair impair impair

impartial impartial impartial

impasse impasse impasse

impassioned impassioned impassioned

impassive impassive impassive

impeccable impeccable impeccable

impecunious impecunious impecunious

impede impede impede

impel impel impel

Practise your weekly spelling words using continuous cursive handwriting

imperative imperative imperative

imperceptible imperceptible imperceptible

imperious imperious imperious

impermeable impermeable impermeable

impervious impervious impervious

impetuous impetuous impetuous

implacable implacable implacable

implausible implausible implausible

implement implement implement

implicate implicate implicate

implicitly implicitly implicitly

impose impose impose

impoverished impoverished impoverished

impregnated impregnated impregnated

impressionable impressionable impressionable

© BT ACADEMY

Practise your weekly spelling words using continuous cursive handwriting

impromptu impromptu impromptu

imprudent imprudent imprudent

impudence impudence impudence

impudent impudent impudent

inaccessible inaccessible inaccessible

inaccurate inaccurate inaccurate

inadequate inadequate inadequate

inadvertently inadvertently inadvertently

inane inane inane

inarticulate inarticulate inarticulate

inattentive inattentive inattentive

inaudible inaudible inaudible

inaugural inaugural inaugural

inaugurate inaugurate inaugurate

inauspicious inauspicious inauspicious

Practise your weekly spelling words using continuous cursive handwriting

incandescent incandescent incandescent

incantation incantation incantation

incendiary incendiary incendiary

incense incense incense

incentive incentive incentive

incessant incessant incessant

incidental incidental incidental

incision incision incision

incisive incisive incisive

incite incite incite

incline incline incline

inclusive inclusive inclusive

incoherent incoherent incoherent

incompetent incompetent incompetent

incongruous incongruous incongruous

Practise your weekly spelling words using continuous cursive handwriting

inconsequential inconsequential inconsequential

inconsistent inconsistent inconsistent

inconspicuous inconspicuous inconspicuous

incorrigible incorrigible incorrigible

incriminate incriminate incriminate

inculcate inculcate inculcate

incumbent incumbent incumbent

indebted indebted indebted

indefinite indefinite indefinite

indeterminate indeterminate indeterminate

indifferent indifferent indifferent

indigent indigent indigent

indignant indignant indignant

indiscernible indiscernible indiscernible

indiscretion indiscretion indiscretion

Printed in Great Britain
by Amazon

34075234R00084